NOBODY'S

HOME

Robert Sherriff

Michael Terence
Publishing

First published in paperback by
Michael Terence Publishing in 2018
www.mtp.agency

ISBN 9781912639335

NOBODY'S HOME

HOME

Robert Sherriff

1

In the Name of the Father

My Father didn't admit to having a past. The story of his early life was a mystery lost in his lack of words and an inability to expose anything that could be vulnerability, humanity or even kindness.

My Mother would eventually and begrudgingly supply me a few details, but this only went on to provoke more questions. He was an enigma to the end; leaving no suicide note, no apology and no peace for those who survived him. I am only certain of one thing. My Father's hate for me was virulent.

The dynamic of the real family is rarely the all-encompassing love of the fairy tale or the softness of the detergent commercial, but my family was extreme by any standards. Violence was our currency and the absence of genuine love left a void that was filled with darkness, betrayal and humiliation. We were an Australian family and Australia was an uncompromising place in the sixties or at least that is how it appeared to me. We were told we were growing up in the lucky country. We were told we could achieve anything through hard work and spirit yet at the same time I was being brutalised and made to feel worthless by the people I loved the most.

It would happen at night. I was small for my age, a premature twin, the smallest to survive in Victoria at the time, I was easily carried out of the house and into the garden by someone of my Father's build. He would be drunk, clumsy and rough. I would be hastily stripped. My clothes were torn from me and I would have to stand defenceless and naked in the yard. I would have to take my chances. I wouldn't wait to see if he would stop at the humiliation and spare me the violence, he never did. I would take advantage of his drunkenness and feel for his grip to loosen or slip and then I would go. I would run through the neighbourhood to escape the attack. Was I worried about the neighbours seeing me naked? Hardly, this had happened so many times before. I knew what it was to run barefoot on cracked bitumen that was baking from the day's biting sun. I knew running naked in the near-freezing winter nights too. I knew what it was like to be running for your life. I spent a childhood running the streets and I've spent a lifetime escaping my Father.

My Father was born in South Australia in 1929. He was the son of a prostitute and born out of wedlock. He must have not known his Father in any meaningful way, but he will have had suspicions about the 100's of men who visited his Mother's house. My Father had inherited a large build, olive skin, deep brown eyes and tremendous capacity for anger. My Father's hair and mood were black for his entire life.

The earliest photograph I have seen of my Father is him as a boy holding a black dog. He had a patience with animals that he was never able to show to people. He was tall and skinny with a mop of black hair. This child would develop into a man of six foot four with a powerful build clothed in skin scarred by the Australian sun. He was mutilated emotionally and carried a pain that could infect anyone in his vicinity. His hands would grow to be huge, always at least twice the size of mine yet he was quite graceful in his movements and well kept. He was clean-shaven and took pride in his appearance. At home, he dressed in casual jeans and shirt and he insisted that they were clean and ironed which meant my Mother would often discover lipstick stains on his collar. A fight would then ensue with the devil rising into those brown eyes and consuming the man.

My Father's childhood was as fractured as any other part of his life. He would always be on the move, change jobs and locations and even personalities but his consistent companions were alcohol and misery. He was Christened Robert Sheriff, the same name he gave me. He left school early and worked a succession of tough, unskilled jobs. He was a station hand and a fruit picker and went from one manual labour to another building callouses and emotional hardness.

The one anecdote I know from his youth is an

incident where he nearly drowned. At age nine he was pulled from the water at Port Pirie. Pirie was and still is a small industrial town in the shadow of grain silos and a lead smelter, about a three-hour drive north of Adelaide where grain shipping and industry had called for unskilled immigrants to come and build a town. All of life in Pirie takes place with the backdrop of the smell of sulphur, a soft scent of hell from the lead smelting process. One day my Father fell into the water that carried the grain ships and plunged toward oblivion in the waters that reflected the belching chimney stacks. A man walking past at the time saw my Father fall and dived into the water to save him. The story made the local press where it describes my Father's saviour as a hero. This stranger's act has ensured thirty-five descendants, I exist because of him, my children and grandchildren, my great-grandchildren, my Sisters, my beloved twin Brother were all offered a chance of life because my Father didn't drown that day but I wonder if my Father had any appreciation for his rescuer and those bitter and soulless years he lived until he decided to meet his maker at his own hands.

Though my Father's history was patchy my memories of my own childhood are not. The site of his near-death became significant for me as a young boy as he took me there to teach me how to swim. Father's lesson involved throwing me off the jetty with a grin on his face. I sunk in the same waters he had, in the shadow of the same industrial chimneys in the run-off of the same toxic processes. I didn't have a hero on the banks poised to save me. I would have to save myself. I had already learned by this stage that I would have to fight to survive him and I swam for the surface and pulled myself out of the water to spite him repeatedly.

I have an image of my Father, when he was outside the house, as a well-dressed man, a man who wore grey pants a white shirt and a two-tone brown and grey jacket that was considered respectable at that time. He was always drinking. He drank West End long necks at breakfast time. He had three cartons at home every week but that was nothing to what he drank in the pub. I think my Mother had tried to get him to cut back once but she was never foolish enough to suggest it again.

Every image I can conjure of him has him glass in hand or glass to lips. People feared him. He dominated every space he entered and other people, even adults, were as affected as me. He had a dark energy; a belligerent nature and he would live life with a dangerous soundtrack of his beloved country music or loud rock and roll. Our house echoed with the sound of Johnny Cash and Hank Williams. It made me hate county music and I'm only starting to get over my aversion now.

The neighbours were always scared of my Father. Wherever we lived he created an empire where his actions were uncriticised for fear of violence and retaliation. All our neighbours witnessed my humiliation plenty of times. They were scared to get involved and even if they witnessed with closed mouths they were greeted with a barrage of snarling and swearing. I know there was an ugly silence around our house and people were witness to horrific crimes without ever speaking up or intervening. I don't carry any resentment for those people. This was a time when men were masters in their own house. It wasn't uncommon for children or wives to be abused and the men who were their abusers to meet the sergeant in the hotel for a quiet word and a pint later. In the early sixties in Australia, there were no safe houses, no campaigns against domestic violence and a belief that a family was a man's property.

I think there was only one occasion when an adult intervened on my behalf. He was called Mr White and I remember that he always wore brown, was six feet six inches, around 240 pounds with blonde wavy hair and couple days of beard growth. He was solid as a shit house that used to be at the back of Auntie Blanche's and Uncle Albert's house. Mr White was briefly my saviour, my man on the shore who saw my fall and dived in to save me. We lived on Hargrave Street in Northfield at the time and Mr White was a neighbour who tired of my Father's version of childcare and belted the crap out of him. The Police arrived just as he was walking due East and we never saw Mr White again.

This was a rare adult intervention on my behalf. An act of violence that didn't teach my Father a thing and didn't save me from further abuse. As I have said I am not angry at the witnesses who didn't come forward or the authorities that didn't protect me. People knew right from wrong but unless you were Mr White you were not armed enough to take my Father on. Justice was only available to the physically strong and more often than not my Father was by far the strongest. My Father was an advocate for the merits of physical strength. He hated my smallness, my frailness and my inability to hurt the same way he could. He systematically set about to teach his children strength and suffering.

He would fill two buckets with water and tell me to stretch my arms out. I knew to do as I was told and despite knowing what was coming, I would always do exactly as he asked. When my arms were out and steady, he would loop the bucket handles over my wrists and demand that I hold then there, straight for as long as I could. I would hold the buckets, my arms screaming with pain, desperate not to disappoint or spark the anger of my Father. He would watch me and justify his actions with the defence that he was driving me to be healthier and more vigorous. This was the start of my Father's torture and it began when I was six years old.

I have other recollections of this early abuse. He had caught me swearing and decided to chastise me to teach me a lesson. He took me outside and removed my trousers and underwear. He then put me over his knee and beat me with a garden hose. The strokes were so violent that I was left with blue and red strokes over my backside and sitting down was impossible for the coming week. These memories are vague and without detail, but I recognise them as the start of patterns of abuse that would culminate in broken bones, emotional damage and a world of hate that not everyone would survive.

My Mother met my Father in 1952. He was working for the RAAF and she told me it was love at first sight. I believe that she did love him before they were married, at that moment when he first arrived in her life and before she really knew him. He was tall and good looking. Her family had been very strict whilst his upbringing was wild and libertarian. She must have seen him as a glamorous escape. In 1953 they married. She told me that all his mates came, and he joined them in getting very drunk. She was appalled but she must have known that alcohol and my Father were synonymous by then. His heritage was beer-soaked with his Mother being a heavy drinker and the addictive gene being passed onto me. I wonder if she knew how tormented her new, young husband was. I wonder what sort of life she had dreamed of and if she thought that my Father could bring her happiness. She could never have known she would die with her husband lost to suicide and her family absent from her bedside.

My Father was twenty-four years old when my Brother, Peter and I were born. My Mother recalled that he was upset by the drive to the hospital to see his new sons. It had been an inconvenience to come to visit and he was happy for her to know it.

I can't remember much of those early years at home with my Mother and Brother but that is no reason to assume they were comfortable or without incident. My Father would often remind me that he had hated me from my birth. He told me that he wished I had never been born or had died in childbirth on many occasions and it was like I had been born into his hatred and lived there my whole life. His particular insult to me was that I was, 'fucking stupid.' He would use that insult for my entire childhood, and it did the damage he required.

My Father's need for destruction was always going to end with his own. We were just lucky he couldn't take us with him. He had been known to come home drunk with a can of petrol and threaten to set himself, the house and us alight. His pain wasn't a personal matter but something everyone else had to pay for. At night I would lie awake waiting for him to come home. I was terrified by the cast of the streetlight outside my room. It would reflect in the dark of his eyes if he came into my room. It would make him look like the demon he was and convince me that this small industrial town was a corner of hell.

He would stalk around the house brooding over something that happened that day, last week, a month ago or not even at all. He would look for his target. My Mother, my Brother, my Sister or me. Then he would punish, seek vengeance. All his misery and hatred and disappointment would be played out on his victim. Often I was that victim, the focus for his spite. Everyone was terrified of this man and I became a scapegoat. My Father once told me he was more frightened of me than I should be of him. Perhaps this is why he reserved a special hatred for me. I can remember his hand around my throat. His thumb on my Adam's apple.

'Four or five seconds of pressure is all it will take,' he would say. Perhaps he was promising to end my pain as well as his.

I know my Mother blamed me for things she did. She stole money and blamed me. She even buried two thousand dollars in the garden once and Dad went over it with the lawnmower. She laid the responsibility with me. She was just trying to avoid another rape or beating.

And so the violence continued. We moved around Australia taking my Father's misery and torture with us. I was beaten by my Father at the pie-cart. I was beaten by him in the street. I was beaten at home. Fists and abuse was the landscape of my childhood as much as the hot dry summers and crabbing down at the jetty. Days out with my Father were tours of the hotels or waiting in the car outside a brothel. Every lesson I learned under his tuition was self-destructive and selfish. The irony was that I still loved that man. He was my Father and I was his son. It would take a particularly brutal assault to give me any chance of escape and once again my rescuers would not be hauling me out of the water but dragging me further under. I wouldn't be able to take a breath for some while.

2

Mother's Love

In defence of my Mother she was a dreamer. I understand that now that I have made it to adulthood. I got through my life by constructing a future where things were better. It was an impossible dream that allowed us to disengage from reality and to survive it. From an early age, she wanted to escape the poverty of her upbringing and the limits of her class. She wanted to be better, different and special. She dreamt of Hollywood and imagined being a singer or a movie actress. She would constantly play records on an old gramophone that I now keep in my current home. We were brought up to the sounds of Al Jolson and my Mother in duet echoing through the house. My Mother would imagine being one of the artists she played, an international superstar.

I think she must have imagined that life for me too and that way she didn't have to acknowledge my reality. In her head, I was with her on the stage. I was famous, rich, happy and she didn't have to feel any guilt. I shared her dreams of being anywhere far away from where I was and inherited her ability to live in a constructed fantasy rather than face the pain of my real life. It is a method for those of us who have very little light. We descend into a darkness where we must imagine stars.

My Mother was born in November 1934. Like my Father, she was born out of wedlock at a time when such things were important. My Mother's, Mother and GrandMother and her Auntie's and Uncles were all born in Victoria to relatively poor families. My Mother told me there was a lot of mental health problems on her Mother's side and instability and chaos would be passed on to her offspring. In her youth, she was a beautiful looking woman; five feet five inches, brown hair, blue eyes, skin like peaches and cream, with a slender build. She was a vibrant person who must have had her fair share of admirers. I expect she had quite a choice if she was prepared to settle for an ordinary working man. My Father wasn't a film star or singer, but he wasn't the pedestrian 'normal' Aussie bloke either. Perhaps that was his appeal.

My Father was the one who brought violence into the house. My Father was a bully, a coward, a drunkard and an abuser. However, my Mother didn't protect me. My Mother didn't defend me. In fact, my Mother would sometimes be responsible for putting me in the path of my Father to defend herself.

I find it difficult to understand and forgive her for the childhood I endured but I do know that she suffered at his hands too and was ill-equipped for the challenge that was leaving him. She was also scared. She suffered both physical and sexual abuse from the beginning of their relationship and this is a time where safe houses and domestic abuse prosecutions were unheard of. Perhaps if my Mother had a better connection with reality, she would never have entertained my Father but finding herself married and pregnant she was content to withdraw into fantasy and let her children take their chances.

My Mother and Father originally put down roots in Victoria and our first home was in a little town called Laverton. We lived in a rustic red brick house with a flat silver roof that reflected the sun, so you could always see our roof from the bottom of the highway. I remember a large lounge and the floorboards that creaked. All the sounds of that time are fearful and ominous. There was the sound of a howling wind out in the backyard that often accompanied my play and there was the sound of my parents fighting from teatime to midnight. It was the backdrop to my early childhood, the score of a horror movie. If my parents had a honeymoon period, then it was well and truly over by the time I was born.

I was born 10-25pm 8th July 1954 in Carlton Hospital, Victoria, one of twin baby boys, my Brother, Peter being born ten minutes later. We were premature, and you could hold us in one hand as we were exactly two pounds each. At that stage, we were the smallest children to ever survive in

Victoria. Mother was only twenty years old. At one stage she would have five children under eight and that was very nearly six if not for my baby Brother's death.

Mother had to go hospital each day to express milk as we were in incubators for months before we could come home. Mother said that Father always complained about driving her to the hospital each day as he was tired from work. We were born into resentment and when we came home, we would have to be fed every three to four hours. Father never ever fed or changed us, so Mother had to deal with two babies on her own because he was working or sleeping.

To give my Mother's story some context you would have to understand Australia in1954. I have said before that Australia was known at this time as the lucky country. We were about to see an economic boom. The Second World War had finished nine years ago; The Korean War had ended the year previously. Everyone was your friend; you did not lock your doors. People would go to the football, cricket, tennis, races and the beach. Life was good; life was fun. Young couples would walk along the beach, hold hands. It was optimistic and innocent. The hotels would shut at 6 pm, and the men (boys) could not drink or vote until they were twenty-one. This was a country built to raise a family, to prosper and live.

My Mother must have felt very outside of this idea

when she brought her children home to a man who hated them. She told me from day one he resented me. She recalls him throwing me around the room. I was the first-born son and the focus for all his rage. I was her little soldier but instead of intervening, she used me to provoke my Father. She admitted to finding ways to torment him, she would tell him she hated him, and his response would be to run riot, scream, rant, punch doors and walls. I was a mummies boy, but my Mother was also lighting the fuse that would explode and end up destroying my childhood.

I must ask myself what she had ever seen in this man. She had such ambition, such aspiration for a better life and when he showed up she must have thought he was her ticket out or at least the best available option.

By the time I was born, I feel she knew what sort of ride she was in for. She knew she was ascending into the twilight zone, a version of hell she could not escape but it was too late to turn back the clock. She had to learn fast how to control those events and when she realises she couldn't have decided that she must at least survive. One of her strategies must have been to sacrifice me.

I remember my Mother would steal out of my Father's wallet and blame it on me. As ridiculous as it sounds, I was the suspect in any theft from about two years old. I had no need or understanding of the pound notes but still, I was the scapegoat. They would fight, and Mother would prime me to be quiet. To not speak about witnessing her helping herself to the money, and this is how she survived. Playing games and pitting family member against family member was her tactic in the war that was our home life.

There was a time when she did intervene in a beating. My Father had been hitting me and she had gone to the kitchen to arm herself with a knife. She told him to leave me alone or she would kill him. My Father then wrestled the knife from her clutches and then turned it on himself. He then had challenged my Mother to push it into him, to kill him. I remember seeing the hate in her eyes and I do remember that she did try to stab my Father but after egging her on to kill him he resisted. I believe she really meant to do it and I know she must have wanted to.

My Mother knew from an early age I would run away. She told me so. When I did run away, I could really take the opportunity to get lost within myself and would pretend my parents were the right people, real people, good people and loving parents. My physical absence made it easier to indulge my emotional absence. I was as lost as she was.

Her real world was full of emptiness. As I grew, she showed less and less pity, less remorse and she tried hard to manipulate all situations to her advantage. She seemed to give up on the real world and only exist in her fantasy. She was unable to stand and protect her children from the beast. She was unable to leave. She would let this monster torture and subject his son to a terrible childhood. Her decision to accept this existence for her son could be read as loyalty to her husband or fear for her life but it was just weakness, a desire to live in fantasy rather than face the truth. Do I hate my Mother for her inability to protect me? No, I love her. She was my Mother.

I have one recollection of her happiness and it came in 1977 at my Father's funeral. I swear that she cried tears of joy. She had survived her marriage to this man.

Near the end of life, my Mother had significant brain aneurysms, and this resulted in the need for major surgery. My Mother could not do anything for herself; and my Sister would wash, change and dress her. I was amazed at how she was still very feisty. My Mother had experienced one of the toughest lives you could. Her body was three-quarters useless and yet she still had spirit. Certainly, my Mother was not a good Mother, but she was a survivor. She had lived a nightmare, withdrawn from it and passed it on to her children but she did manage to retain part of herself in doing so.

I did not go to my Mother's funeral. I was told of her death sometime after it happened. I did bring my Mother's ashes back to my house though. I walked through the front door and the hairs stood up on my neck. Above my bed was a picture of Paris with the Eiffel tower prominent. That day my Wife had been to buy a quilt set and had returned with the pillows cases and cover each having the same picture of the tower on them. My Mother had come home in a box with exactly the same image on. Was my Mother trying to communicate with me from the grave? Was it coincidence? It may have just been a reminder of how we had both survived by creating similar fantasies.

I was left shaking and all the memories of childhood came rushing back to overwhelm me. I started to float, leave my body and engage all the coping strategies I had created to survive my childhood.

None of us escape unscathed in the end.

3

Boiling Point

Our unhappy family suffered tragedy in Victoria. My parents had gone on to have another son two years after I and my twin were born, and he had died. I recall him as a happy, healthy baby with three teeth and I remember trying to stir him from his sleep and his refusal to wake up. I was the one who found my precious little Brother lifeless and I always felt there was a lot of anger towards me from my Father as if my discovery was somehow linked to responsibility. Perhaps my face just carried a reminder of the pain of losing a child. I just knew I felt my grief at the loss and a little extra too. I also always had doubts about my Mother's possible involvement. She was tired, broken and struggling with the children she already had. Was it impossible that she snapped?

My parents were left with three sons and one daughter and in 1960 they packed us into a car and moved us to South Australia. The journey would take two weeks with Father drinking heavily and then driving in short bursts. The destination was Port Pirie where his Mother lived. As far as I know, the move was prompted by a combination of a few things. Father had enough of his job, and he wanted to be around extended family. We didn't ask for any sort of reason and spent the journey staring out of the car window or waiting for him to wake or sober up so we could get on the move again.

Pirie is still a tough industrial town. It's probably changed very little since my arrival. I recall my first sight of the landscape and the skyline being dominated by the huge wheat silos as we hit town. There was also the smell of the lead smelter, the air always with its ominous touch of sulphur. This was the setting for the most significant event in my young life and my descent into a personal hell. I didn't know what I was in for, but I wasn't naïve enough to think life was going to be wonderful from now on.

Moving to Pirie did give us the opportunity to be around family. My grandMother and great grandMother lived there, and I had aunts and uncles. We could have had freedom and a simple childhood with a wide circle of connected adults. I wasn't convinced by the idea of an extended family, a community where I could grow in a safe and supportive environment. I'm not sure what fantasy my Mother was moving to, but I had developed a sort of cynicism. I was already a damaged child. I would pinch myself, hit myself and leave bruises over my body. I would like to bang my head hard and try and hurt myself. I would hide under my bed when things got tough. If anybody had looked at me, they would have seen that I was not a happy, normal young boy.

I do remember playing out in the garden at the house in Pirie with my Brother and twin, Peter. I did have some simple childhood pleasures and all these happy childhood memories are populated by Peter and me. We lived behind a bakery on Swift street and occasionally we would get treats from the baker. He would give us cakes and biscuits and we would be at the height of luxury and indulgence eating the sweetness out in the garden. I also remember my one and only time on a horse when I and Peter had mounted one briefly in a field before it galloped off and ejected us over a fence.

The street was still old-fashioned housing with outside toilets and little in the way of real luxury or modernity but to my young mind it was an exciting, vibrant place as there was a siren from the smelter that sounded every hour on the hour and we could hear it from our house. The good memories are rare, and those times are hard to recall. Pirie didn't offer me any more of a childhood that Victoria had done.

I was already terrified of my Father. I would shake, wet myself and even shit myself in his company. I did not know exactly why I was so scared but later my Mother told me about incidents with cigarette butts held on my arms and legs when I had been younger in Victoria. Even if I hadn't retained all the details of what he did he was still a figure who promised pain and fear and I knew that he had a dislike for me.

That day started like most days with my Father going to the hotel. It was early in the summer of 1961. He was working on the railways at the time but must have taken some time off to go drinking. Some of his friends from the RAAF had come over from Victoria to visit for the week. Mother thought that he might have been playing cards and lost a lot of money. He came back to the house with a smirk on his face and immediately embarked on a sustained beating that would cost me bones and teeth.

I was in the back yard playing. I remember it as a sunny day. I think I remember him coming into the house. I would have said, 'Hello Rob.' As I never called him dad.

He called us all into the house and all of us kids were assembled in front of him. He was swearing and punching the walls and shrieking like a lunatic. My siblings were faster than me and took to their heels to escape. My Father managed to catch hold of me and declared that if anyone tried to help me he would kill them.

The attack was ferocious and epic, my Father's masterpiece of domestic violence. Other family members have described the events of that day spanning as much as seven hours. During my assault Mother had time to save the other children by taking them through a gap in the fence to a neighbour. My uncles had also tried to intervene and showed up at our house, but my Father had said that if they went to my aid he would kill me.

It would take the arrival of eight policemen to finally halt the attack but by that point, I had lost teeth and armed with a broomstick Father had broken my arm and four ribs.

He was a drunk, snarling mess and even as he was restrained by the police, he was still screaming that he was going to kill me. I called him a bastard that day and when I did, he spat at me. The police began to hit him but even that didn't wipe the look from his face.

When the police had arrived at the house I had been hiding under the bed. I was covered in shit and piss, shaking and refusing to come out. I was seven years old. It took the police close to an hour to talk me out from my refuge. My Mother was also trying to get me to emerge, but I ignored her, avoided her touch and wouldn't respond to her at all. When I did come out it was to the arms of a policeman. I had more faith in the treatment I would get from a uniformed stranger than anyone in my immediate family.

The police took me to the hospital then back to the Police station where they stripped me of all my clothes and took photos of me naked. I then went back to the Hospital. The photos were to be used as evidence but in the end, were considered too horrific to share.

My Mother told me in the latter years that she had

never seen me so scared before and that I was as white as a ghost. I told her I had been scared every day of my life.

A Police Officer held me all the way to the hospital and then back to the Police Station and then back to the Hospital. These officers may have had children of my age and may even go home to them that evening after dealing with the effects of my Father's evil on his child. I imagine it was a very difficult day at work for them.

I was worried about my Brothers and Sisters. I did not know at that stage they were next door, safe, away from my Father. I didn't know whether they had suffered the same or even worse than me.

That evening I lay delirious in hospital shaking and crying and even calling out for my parents. I was still able to hero-worship my parents not because I loved them, them me or because they had any good qualities but because I was able to construct a fantasy about who they were. In my semi-conscious state, I was calling out for my fantasy Mother and Father; the good strong man and the loving, nurturing woman. When I did become fully conscious and found my Mother there, I began to scream, and the hospital eventually removed my Mother to stop me the distress. There was a court order to keep my Father away, but I was so traumatised that the approach of any adult would make me shake and wet the bed. I trusted nobody, but the nurses were patient. They washed me, held me, let me sleep with the light on and would be there to comfort me when I cried. For a long time, I was in a great deal of physical pain and my body was battered and bruised.

I spent one week in the Pirie hospital and then was sent to live with a policeman and his family while arrangements were being made. It took me a long time to recover physically from the broken bones and I'm not sure I knew exactly what would happen to me but for this time I was part of a normal family. There was a happiness for me here. The family were kind and had children my age too, but I knew it was temporary and that the family life I was experiencing was never going to be rightly mine. The police had notified the community welfare department about the incident and they wanted to make my Brothers and Sister wards of state. It would mean my family was to be monitored by the department and visited for the next four years. The consequences for me would be more significant.

The attack cost my Father the love of his family. His Mother and grandMother never forgave him. A lot of his friends were now able to see the type of man he was at home, the true him and they withdrew not liking who they saw. My Father was sacked from his job and this began his cycle of job after, job, after job, of failure and blown chances.

The judge wanted to jail my Father. He described him as a vicious creature. I still have the cutting from the local paper with the judge's quote. My Father had also admitted to two other counts of violence against me. It turned out that he had been arrested for violence against me on two previous occasions in South Australia. My Mother pleaded to the judge for leniency perhaps for his sake or perhaps for herself. She pointed out that he was the breadwinner and that she had given birth to my baby Sister and that she had other children to support. The judge heard her appeals and fined my Father fifty pounds. This was a lot of money in 1961 and it would have caused the family great hardship to pay it.

I recovered my physical health whilst in the care of the police, but I was far from undamaged. My ability to trust, to love to know happiness was starting to erode and at seven years old I needed support and so the authorities decided that I needed to be removed from my family and placed in the safety of the state.

I was driven by three policemen to the Glandore Boys' Home and I'm sure they thought they were delivering me from evil. I was to be protected from my Father and placed in the care of professionals who had the experience to bring up a fragile little boy.

Out of the frying pan...

4

Glandore

I was a victim of my Father and a victim of the state. I know the moment where I was changed forever, and it happened at Glandore Boys' Home. The home was founded in 1869 and went through a few name changes, including Edwardstown Industrial School, until it shut in 1973. I knew it as Glandore, but it might as well have been hell. It was run in a military-style with order and discipline used as a cover for brutality. We had weekly haircuts, domestic duties and regular inspections. We were being taught to be clean, respectful, obey rules and to keep our mouths shut. Above all, we needed to keep our mouths shut.

I will always remember the day my innocence was stolen. I was seven years old. Although I had just been through the most disturbing and grotesque experience in my family home at the hands of the people I most loved, trusted. I still looked up to my parents. I still loved my parents; it did not matter what they did. I loved them and wanted them back.

Every night I was away from my parents I fretted. I was worried about them. I was still loyal to my family, my blood. I missed my twin Brother. He had been my companion for seven years. I had never been apart from him.

I would cry all night, loudly and vigorously. I would scream and sob. On my first day in the home, I had showered in the morning with the other boys. One of the older boys had punched me and I had run out of the building naked and wet. There was a nurse there, a kind adult who had wrapped me in a towel and comforted me. I'm sure if she had known what was in store for me, she might have told me to keep running.

John Bartlett started at Glandore Boys' Home in 1955 as the third most senior officer.

He was a very tall man, solid build; he looked like a bear. His hands were quite big, and he had dark black hair and deep, dark brown eyes. He was in his mid-30's. Bartlett had a son at Glandore. The boy had been born with cerebral palsy. There was an incident where I had seen Bartlett deal with his upset son by beating him into silence. He was from the same school of childcare as my Father. It was John Bartlett who first sexually assaulted me.

I can recall the incident. There was a shed between the kitchen office and the school. It was windowless, dark. Outside the sun was gleaming and a large adult cast a shadow over me, his face blacked in silhouette. I was scared, terrified. I was so aware of my heart racing and my limbs trembling as I was escorted from the daylight into the dark recess. I started to feel an out of body experience coming on. There was a golden light flooding over me. I now recognised the face of the dark figure. It was John Bartlett. I saw him perfectly, clearly, I still see him to this day.

I was stripped. My shoes, undies and singlet taken away. I began to scream, and a hand was put over my mouth. I couldn't breathe. I was gasping, struggling to suck in air. I was suspended, limp in the grasp of this man.

Afterwards, I was lying on the ground in the foetal position. I put my hand to my bum and brought it back covered in blood and shit. It smelt terrible. I thought of my Mother and Father. They would have killed John Bartlett. As much as they had hurt me, they would have stopped this, surely. I was in shock, the experience, the blood on my hands. I had changed in that moment. At first, I had felt great pain but as I endured what happened I became numb. I became like the other boys. We were in a war zone and we couldn't win. We had to withdraw into ourselves and pray for survival.

There was a cast of adult characters at Glandore, some good, some bad but all must have suspected or even known what was happening. There was an air of brutality about much of what happened day-to-day.

Vern Beard was the headmaster of the school for roughly forty years. He was in charge when I attended. He was a very imposing figure with an 18th-century beard. He loved the cane and from time to time would use a ping pong bat on the backs of hands or even bare arses.

He would often appear when we were in the showers and stand to stare at our naked bodies especially the genitals. All of the boys called him 'The Pig'.

Jim Slade was the Superintendent. He was a short man, bald a little fat who wore glasses. Mr and Mrs Slade had no children of their own. Mrs Slade was beautiful. Mrs Slade thought of us as hers sometimes whilst her husband loved the cane too. When he canned you, he gave it everything he had and sweat would drip down his face.

Nurse Flaherty smoked all the time. I remember her from Day one at the Boys Home; she was kind caring above all a Nurse. She was there if every I hurt myself, she always had lots of Band-Aids. She had yellowish golden hair that was long and curly. I remember her teeth were like the shark's teeth you see in Jaws movies. Her eyes were open very wide all the time. I don't think I have seen anyone else look like this. She was a character and had the most infectious laugh.

Don Craig was the second most senior officer at Glandore Boys' Home. Don was tall six foot plus, late 40's with a moustache that he would curl and he had a very slight humped back. He would flirt with all the female staff and the boys liked him.

Mr Craig taught me this saying;

(I complained because I had no shoes until I meet a man who had no feet)

And then there are the others, the faceless and nameless men who became part of my Glandore experience and taught me nothing but hate.

There was the man in his fifties who walked with a cane. He liked to grab the boys by their penises and if you resisted, he would give you a beating. Then there was the skinny guy with a big nose who would have his hands all over you. He had a voice a little like Bugs Bunny. My whole time at Glandore was punctuated by brutal acts of abuse by adults and even some of the older boys and those abusers were confident that nobody would stop them.

It was early on at Glandore that I found out about death. I remember seeing a dead bird on the ground and another boy explaining that the bird had now gone to heaven. Even at that age, the idea of death appealed to me. I had fantasies about being wrapped up in a blanket and shut in a box. I was warm, safe from the outside world. I wouldn't exist so nobody could harm me.

I became excellent at living in a fantasy world. Disassociation became my normal state of being at Glandore. I perfected within those walls as a means of survival. I was a victim, but I wasn't the only victim. This was an institution run on the abuse of those nobody cared about, devils put in charge of the most vulnerable and most voiceless children.

At Glandore, I made friends with a boy named

Trevor. We were both seven years old and we formed a bond in that hell which kept us going. Trevor was taller than me with red hair and light brown eyes. Trevor was a ward of state too. We used to dorm together, play together and even shower together. I remember running along the tram line with him and on occasion, we even managed to persuade the milkman or baker for free goodies to share. At night we would lie out on the oval and look at the stars. Trevor and I once took an extra bowl of porridge at breakfast and Slade gave us one hell of a canning. The memory is so vivid it is like it was yesterday. Trevor, my friend, my blood Brother. I have tried to find out what happened to him. I saw him when we were twelve years old. He was behind a window and we were forbidden to speak. We both cried. I asked the police to see if there was any trace of him. He had disappeared, left no records of his existence at Glandore. How can somebody just disappear? Glandore will probably never give up all its secrets and all I can do is tell my story and curse the brutes who preyed on me.

5

Angels and Demons

I have lived a life of dreams and nightmares for fifty-six years now. I must accept that much of the man I am is because of that little boy lost, because of Bartlett, my Father and the others who preyed upon my vulnerability. Of course, I am also the boy who survived all that and made it through to adult life. I had the resources, the skills and the luck to live long enough despite my attempts to take another path. I will tell you about the suicidal feelings and actions that were part of my life and how it is a minor miracle that I'm still here to tell this story but first I will explain how as a child I coped with the abandonment and abuse I had to endure.

Dissociation for survivors of childhood sexual abuse may include feelings of confusion, disorientation, nightmares, flashbacks, difficulty experiencing emotions and the inability to form proper relationships. I experienced all of this and I moved through life using denial and repression as a mask for my pain.

Then, out of nowhere, my demons would strike back and send me sprawling to the ground. All the isolation, the pain, doubts that linger would overwhelm me and plunge me back into the darkness. From very early in my life I was like a vessel into which characters and personalities could be stored to bring out in times of need. This cast of characters would be my fantasy escape, my safety net when reality was threatening to overwhelm me.

Henry is a seven-year-old boy. He is good company, funny, bright. I still have the company of Henry up to this day. Then there is Harvey. He was such a funny character too. He took over when I was a ten-year-old. He would fight my battles. Any of the fights I got into at school or Glandore Boys' Home, Harvey would fight for me. Harvey won a few. I lost a lot. There are others, Ben is a character reminiscent of the song that Michael Jackson wrote for his rat.

This cast of characters stand shoulder to shoulder with me as I continue to face my nightmares. I have this reoccurring dream where everything is an opaque black and I can see are the outline figure of a male adult reaching out to the boy to grasp the child's hand. The child can't speak as his lips are sewn together. I know it's me even though I cannot see the face of the child. I can hear a muffled noise and the sound of a whimpering cry and the wind begins to rise. Then there follows a deafening crash of thunder and I would hear this voice say, 'trust me, believe me,' This adult was holding my hand. I could not get free.

From an early age, I suffered complex trauma and

this affected my developing brain. I have, as an adult, to comprehend it and accept it, and it may have limited my capacity to integrate sensory, emotional and cognitive information, which then leads to over-reactive responses to subsequent stress and long-term effects such as cognitive, behavioural, physical and mental health problems. I have often suffered from fits of delirium, but I believe the dissociation to have been a useful weapon or at least shield to help me to survive my childhood.

My ego structure was overwhelmed by the experience of the sexual abuse and I learned from an early age to leave my body. I could remove myself from the experience and that way does not carry the true horror of it. Of course, that pain and hurt was never truly escaped but logged away so that it would drip feed and bleed out throughout my life and it would fuel the self-destructive behaviour for years to come.

From an early age, I was using razor blades to cut myself. I would go and hide in the toilet and cut pieces of my hands and arms. I would have been about ten-years-old when this started. I was trying to hurt them, the adults that hurt me, but I took it out on myself. I did it every second day. I would need stitches. The adults around me could not work out why I was mutilating myself. I'm not even sure if I knew at the time. I know now, and I still have some of the scars on my hands to this day.

When my Father hurt me, I could see what was happing. I would float around the room like white feathers from a pillow, light and soft and warm. I was outside my body wondering if my Father was from a different planet. Both of us were alien and otherworldly.

It is scary sometimes I see myself falling from the sky spinning around and around in circles, spinning out of control there is nothing for me to grab on to. The air passes through my hair I am in free flight. My hand, my face, my ears, and my nose were all freezing up. I then would hit the ground with the loudest, biggest thud. Where there was dust rising past me. Exploding ten feet into the air. I struggle to get up off the ground, and the dust is still swirling all around me. Like a mini-tornado dancing round and round.

The self-destructive behaviour, the cutting, the dissociation was my sanctuary all the time I was at Glandore and even when I was sent home for visits. The staff were concerned enough to send me for tests and treatments, and I was beginning to be scared of myself too.

They made me have lots of EEG. I think they were trying to work out if I was just naughty or crazy? They gave me these tests after the test. They then started me on so many medications that would make me tired all the time. I would always go to sleep in class. I was like a zombie. I would then get the cane from Mr Beard. They were always sending me to all sorts of Doctors to find out what was wrong with me but of course, many of them knew exactly why I was so disturbed.

Then there were the cards they showed me. And the pictures they asked me. What do they mean? How was I supposed to know? They were always doing some tests on me and giving me new medication each time. I at this point was hearing sounds and voices. Voices that would be calling me.

As an adult, I once told a doctor all I saw at night was Blood. I told him about my other bad dreams as well. There were scenarios where lights would flicker and flash in a passageway in which I was running fast. I always would be looking behind me for that dark shadow. A shadow from my past. The past where I could never escape from. Where I would be hunted down and killed.

I now know that I most likely would have been diagnosed as ADHD if there was a name for it back in the early '60s. I was scattered, disembodied and if I spoke, I would jump from subject to subject. I was shattered at their hands.

I was to become a tool in this toxic orchestra, their instrument to do as they please with 24/7. No wonder I constructed so many creative ways to survive.

What I loved to do as a child was to create an image, I lay on my back at Glandore on the oval and look at the night sky. I would imagine what it would be like to ride a falling star, as it flicker's, shine's, and it glows in the evening sky.

I have always known I had a Guardian Angel. I have always known that there was a force protecting me. How could I have survived so much time with the devil if there wasn't somebody giving me divine support?

6

Sister of Mercy

My Sister was born in August 1955 at Carlton
Victoria. My twin Brother, I and my Sister were
incredibly close. We were the three Musketeers, all
for one and one for all. We were very rarely apart,
and we formed a little unit outside the adults. By
the time my Brother, and I had reached five my
Sister was taller than us and she would use her
physical superiority to let us know she was in
charge but we both loved her still.

My Sister had short golden-white wavy hair and
blue eyes. She had been blessed with very a loud
voice and boy could she scream. Her angelic looks
and her sweet nature meant that she was a child
who people always seemed to like. She would
always be the centre of attention when there was a
crowd but not from dominating and being an
extrovert but from being demure and polite. The
expression 'butter would not melt in her mouth' was
coined for my Sister. Of course, this angel of a child
would quite happily bash her 'little' Brothers to get
her own way.

My Sister's early life and her apparent softness
contrast with the terrible voyage she would have to
endure. My Sister was to experience a life I

wouldn't wish on anyone and it hardened her. She became a strong woman. It was the only way she could survive.

By the time I was twelve I had spent five years going back and forth from Glandore Boys' Home to my family. This time was also punctuated by time with foster carers and other relatives, but I spent the majority of my childhood cowering from the abuse of the boy's home or trying to survive my Father.

I was around the age of 12 or 13 when I spent some of the winter in the family home in Adelaide. It was another of those uneasy times where the family was united, and I was happily away from Glandore and in the relative security of ordinary domestic abuse. One night I remember being woken by the sound of crying. I recognised the sound of my Sister's distress and called out to her.

'Sis. Are you alright?' I called out again from my bed but there was no response.

The crying lasted a while and there was no answer to my calls. I decided that I would get up and see what was going on. I shared a room with my twin Brother so I tiptoed across to him to see if I could wake him. I told him our Sister was crying but now she had gone silent. I desperately wanted him to go and investigate or at least to accompany me. I tried to persuade him to go as my anxiety began to grow. I felt that warm feeling in my groin and then run down my legs. I was conditioned to be scared and wetting myself was a common occurrence.

I stood there pleading with my Brother to help me. Without his support, I decided to go and wake Mother and Father so they could find out the reason for my Sister's distress. I remember the combined force of the moonlight and the streetlight burning through the window. It was a full moon and it was casting shadows that terrified me; shadows that were reminiscent of the shed at Glandore and the darkness that had descended over me there.

Outside the window, the wind was howling. I could hear the trees rustling moving back and forth in the yard. Hail had already woken me twice that evening and the rain continued to drive at the windows. The storm raged outside and built into thunder and lightning as I braced myself to leave the security of my room and go to my Sister's aid. I decided that I would head straight to her so I opened the door and began to sneak, on tiptoe, to her room.

When I opened her bedroom door I was confronted by the shadow. At first, I could not make out what or who I was seeing so I turned the light on, and I then saw my Father.

My Father had blood all over his right hand, and he was naked. I cried out to Mother.

'Sleep, sleep child.' was her reply.

I screamed that my Father had killed my Sister I

then ran, as fast as I could out the front door. I banged on our next-door neighbour's house I and carried on screaming that my Father had murdered my Sister begin the occupants to call the police.

I was crying and shaking, and it was so cold, and I was soaking wet with urine and shivering from my terror.

I continued to stutter, 'Please call the police. Help her.'

I don't know how long I was outside, but the neighbours eventually woke up and took me in. They bathed me and put me in one of their spare beds. Later I remember the police did come and they asked me for a statement. I told them what I had experienced, everything I could remember. I still thought that my Father had killed my Sister and that my Mother had let him do it. I knew my Father had come to the neighbour's door, but I had actually felt quite safe at that point. I knew my Father could not hurt me as the lady next door had two sons and they were bigger than him.

The two boys had gone over to my house after I had turned up on their doorstep. They had knocked on the door and my Father told them to fuck off. Then my Father had thrown my Brothers, Sisters and Mother out of the house and into the street. It was my Mother and our neighbours who had then called the police.

My Father was arrested and locked up for three years. His Mother died while was in jail. He did not go to the funeral.

It was during this prison stint that I began to take advantage of his absence. I probably thought I was free and was unaware that I was acting out from the damage he had caused.

I had access to his car and I would drive it all over Adelaide. I was only 12 or 13 but already I was picking up girls going on dates. I would take them to drive-in movies. Another favourite spot was Saint Kilda Beach as there was unlikely to be any police there. As I said, I began to live my own life, but I wasn't aware that I was still in my Father's shadow.

My Sister eventually moved to the top end of Australia where she now lives with Aboriginal people. She has been there for the last four years and it seems to have done her good.

She seems to have mellowed and is able to forget the past. I know she is a different person from the damaged young girl my Father left behind. She now speaks in a very low voice. She now has a softness about her. Peace. She has lost that hardness she had developed to stay alive. We were so close as young kids, so open. We had lost that to survive and even shut ourselves off from each other.

I can never understand my Mother rolling over and making out she was asleep? Why hadn't she have ever helped my Sister? Why hadn't she protected my Sister, her child, and not turned her back on her, abandoned her to suffer sexual attacks from my Father? My Father had, on many occasions. raped my Mother in front of me. I was a child, but I knew enough that I could tell he was hurting my Mother. I didn't understand the nature of sexual assault until I was older, until I was able to identify my own victimhood along with hers. I came to understand the sickness of the rapist, the power and damage of that evil and I feel blessed that I was never that evil.

My Mother, unsurprisingly, took my Father back the second he left prison. She took him back and continued to turn a blind eye to the suffering of my Sister. The attacks continued until she, and my other Sister, were able to move out. Whilst the attacks went on all three women were silent and protected themselves by protecting my Father. They had no sort of life and I am amazed how they were able to live through what they did and go on to have families of their own.

They both went on to have children themselves, even grandchildren now and to the outside, these families might seem quite normal and free of shadows that we had to endure. This is just a surface impression. I know that my Sister's oldest child, my nephew, is also the child of my Father.

7

Inferno

From the age of eleven, my life had become a circular journey between Port Pirie, The Boy's home and Northfield in South Australia. I was already damaged and desperate from the sexual and violent attacks that dominated my young life. My Father continued to drink and discharge his pain my way. My Mother continued to facilitate her children's destruction. I was primed and ready to detonate.

My Mother was also grooming me to be a career criminal by this stage. It began with a con that we would play at the delicatessen or market. I was small, angelic-looking and I would fill my basket with bread, cans of food, meat and treats for my siblings and self. Pulling my most innocent expression I would assure the shopkeeper that my Mother would be along soon with the money to pay and most times I would be allowed to leave the shop with everything I could carry. My Mother would be waiting for me out of sight.

Later, when I was living on the streets of Adelaide, I was an expert in getting hold of free and high-quality food. My apprenticeship lasted for the whole time the family lived in Northfield and my Brothers and Sisters were schooled there too.

Adelaide reminded me of the Southern States of America. The place was 50 years behind the Eastern and Western States of Australia, a backwater town. We were the cowboys in Adelaide. When we moved from Port Pirie, we lived at Sturt Street Adelaide for twelve months and this is where I would learn the craft of a street kid. We lived in a place with two bedrooms. There were two adults and five children. It is while we lived at Sturt Street Adelaide my Mother and I would branch out into all sorts of theft. We robbed jewellers and coin shops, the places you could steal from and then sell these goods to hock shops or pawn shops.

My Mother would always stand at the entrance of the store. I always went to the opposite side. I would carry a bag and get on my knees or lay on the floor. I would pretend I was reading a book. When the shopkeeper was distracted, I would then slowly go to the other end of the counter where there would be a small door you could push open. I would then put my arm around the corner and open the cupboard and steal, steal, steal. We would walk out with handfuls of jewellery to sell. This would feed us and support my Father to drink. On the surface, I accepted this as my life but inside I was burning with rage and about to self-destruct.

A lot of things I learned in the family helped me out when I was a street kid. I found places to sleep at the central markets and the train station, big buildings with small doors that opened to car parks, cars that had the property that I could hock. Often when I went to these pawn shops, they did not care what I was selling or who owned the property. Stealing became a major part of my life.

I became an expert at it. I could take over two hundred dollars' worth a day of food and property and cash. I would not starve. I did not have to work for a wage. I was making double what the average salary would have been. I was even given my Father money to keep him in his lifestyle. Of course, I knew it would backfire. More money meant more drink and more hidings.

There was milk money left out at houses during the night often under the front door mat, bread money, during the day, often left in letterboxes and newspaper money all the time.

My Father tried to tell me off for stealing so I said to him as I was running off out the door. 'You asked me to do that so did Mother.' What could he say? They gave me no choice, every time I went somewhere, I was stealing, often for them. I was learning how to play their game now. My Father would waste all his money on horse's, women and alcohol. My Father would go to Hotels and drink big three times a week. While in and out of Glandore Boys' Home I would take trolleys of food home to feed my Brothers and Sisters. I was the provider. I soon became street smart, proud of what I could do but all the time I still knew it was wrong, still knew I was being used and abused and eventually the real horror of my life would catch up with me.

I must have been twelve-years-old when there was an incident that first provoked my rage. We were living at Hargrave Street Northfield. I was also periodically on the streets as well at this stage, as well as being sent back and forth to Glandore Boys' Home.

I do not know or can't remember exactly all the details that happened on this day, but I do know. I could have been charged with murder. The violence, the sexual abuse, the sadness and pain threatened to overwhelm me. I was suicidal and had no wish to survive. I knew that death offered a release from my suffering and at the time it seemed to be the only way out. This time it wasn't my Father hitting me but my Mother. She was holding a length of wood and striking me repeatedly. I could feel the blows, but I could also feel this build-up of pressure in my head and heart. The kettle was about to boil and force a high-pressure jet of steam out of me.

It was the first time I ever experienced this level of rage. My Mother rained blows on to me and as usual, I was crying, screaming and pleading. As usual, the neighbours would have been able to hear my torment. It was daytime and then could have just looked over the garden fence to see a woman thrashing a child with a weapon. Nobody was going to come to my aid, but I didn't lie down this time and accept my fate.

I found myself armed with an axe. I was backing

away from my Mother, but I was brandishing it to protect myself. For the first time in this battle, I was armed. It all happened in slow motion like I was a spectator to a weird dream. Then almost instantly I regained control and I was back in my body. I dropped the axe to the floor and fell to my knees.

I was screaming, 'Kill me, kill me.'

I looked up, and my Mother was visibility shaken and crying as well. The neighbour's son had appeared and was pinning me to the ground. I continued screaming, crying, swearing. I had no control. I had no life. I had no hope. I needed someone to hold my hand, to kill me now. I wanted no more of this life. Fuck it. Get away from me. Shoot me. No one loves me. No one will cuddle me or tell me I was loved, and I was not a loser. And you know who held me and wiped my tears and told me she loved me it was Mrs S, the neighbour who had sent her son to restrain me. I don't know what she had seen but she was kind and brave enough to come to the aid of a raging, angry, scared boy who was swinging an axe. She knew the life I had.

The Police came and took me to Glandore Boys' Home. I did not see my Mother for another three months. I will always see that day as a turning point in my life. I knew I came close to hurting my Mother. It would have been so different if I hadn't gained control. Perhaps I would be the villain in someone's story. Perhaps I would be remembered as the monster.

The fact remains that despite my rage and despite my pain, I didn't ever lash out and destroy my Mother. I came close but I had something my Father didn't – a conscience. Even when I didn't care whether I lived or died I didn't have it in me to hurt people. I was and would remain just a scared little boy.

8

Back in Anger

On the 16th January 1966, I was returned to Glandore Boys' Home where I remained barring holidays and placements until 20th December 1968. I was twelve years old and was back in the 'care' of the state because my Mother had me arrested. I had been taken by the police to their headquarters in Adelaide and then on to Glandore. I knew what was waiting for me there and if I had the chance to go on the run I would have taken it.

The same staff were waiting for me at the boy's home, the same monsters but with one new addition; Mr Don Craig. He was a funny man and we affectionately named him Mr Giggle-Pot, which as Glandore nicknames went was the best you could hope for.

On my return, I discovered that the Aboriginal lads were now playing good football and they had just won final for that grade and year. It was the little bit of unity and pride we really needed to survive, and we cheered them on. Glandore boys were good at something finally, had some minor success to cling to and a distraction from the day to day menace of the predatory staff.

At the turn of the year, I came down with

tonsillitis. It was a brutal attack and put me in the sickbay for a few days. The weather was hot, and the nurses treated me and my fever by plunging me naked into ice baths on regular occasions. I can still feel the shock of hitting the water and the relief of being allowed to climb out.

I was the only boy in sickbay at the time. I must have been too good an opportunity to miss. It was dark in the room as the curtains were closed to protect against the summer sun. It was also probably evening when I woke.

Bartlett was on my bed, a shadowy figure but unmistakably him sat looking at me whilst I had been asleep.

I only had time to comprehend where I was and who was with me before he placed his hand over my mouth. The other hand went under the blanket. He sat there stifling my cries and groping me in silence. I could hear the deepness of his breaths and see that he was sweating and shaking a little too. All of the time he was abusing me his eyes were darting about the room to check for danger, for an interruption to his attack.

As I lay there the rage started to build again and I started to struggle, to try and pull my body away from or to turn on my back. My internal voice was screaming, 'No. Fuck this shit. This isn't happening again.'

Meanwhile, Bartlett kept his hand over my mouth and his grip on my prick and was panting and sweating. My inner anger had no way out. I wasn't strong enough to even get a sound out into the room let alone physically escape. Bartlett was a big man, and I feared him. I had seen how he dealt with his own son and I had been bloodied and broken by him in the shed and pretty soon I realised how vulnerable and powerless I was.

I tried to escape the only way I could. I tried to ignore his heavy breathing and slow my own down, to disengage from the rhythm of the attack and the physical power of this man. I wanted to escape my body, to disassociate, to survive.

After Bartlett stopped fondling me, he just got up and left. He didn't say anything and of course, I didn't tell anyone about that incident because I was too frightened. The nurse came in the following morning and I was sobbing. She knew I was heartbroken, but I couldn't tell her anything about why.

My tonsillitis wasn't quick to improve, and I spent a whole two weeks in the sickbay. Isolated and out of sight from other staff and boys I was easy picking for Bartlett, and he would visit regularly and become more daring each time.

Eventually, Bartlett was masturbating me and himself regularly and his furtive looks around the room disappeared as he became more confident and brazen about his abuse. He had a captive victim, one who was out of sight and too scared to talk and he was going to make the best of it.

Even after I left sickbay and started to recover from my illness Bartlett still had his fixation with me and would always single me out for special treatment.

Sometime later I was recovered and laying in my bed. Bartlett would have had to use the darkness to sneak through the dining area and past the office to get to me, but he appeared once again sat on the edge of my bed. Instead of lying still and letting him get his hand over my face this time I bolted as soon as I was aware of his presence. I ran for the bathroom and he ran after me. I must have hoped he wouldn't follow because once in the bathroom I was trapped, and I collapsed onto the floor sobbing.

Tears were already flowing, and I was shaking. As he entered, I begged him to leave me alone. It was a simple plea, 'Please don't hurt me.' It was all I had, and I knew it was worthless.

My attempted escape seemed to aggravate him, so he just grabbed me by the hair and began to rip at my clothes. He was a fully grown and big man and I was a very slight twelve-year-old and once again I was totally at his mercy, but my vain resistance would be met with increased brutality this time.

He held me close to him as he dropped his trousers and sat on the toilet seat. He groped me and began his heavy breathing close enough, so I could feel the flow of his breath. I was uncontrollably shaking and sobbing so he placed his hand around my throat and tried to choke a silence and stillness into me. I believed he was going to kill me this time and I started to float away, to try and leave reality and my body. I repeated the word 'don't' repeatedly, a futile mantra that wouldn't stem the horror.

He spans me around and forced me to sit down on his lap. I could feel his erection against my backside and his breath on my neck. I kept on struggling. I was trying to scream so he put his hand over my mouth again and growled at me to, 'shut the fuck up.'

I managed to get myself off his lap and fell forward onto the floor and there he pinned me between his legs. I was done, completely out of fight and overwhelmed by his strength. There I remained until I felt his warm semen land on my back.

Bartlett made me shower and make my bed.

I never said a word to anyone about what Bartlett did to me. He would continue to prey on me, to single me out for the cane when we were in the company of the other boys and sexual attacks in private. When we used to pass each other in the corridor or yard there was a sick energy between us, a sort of electric hatred that made us shake. He was my nemesis and tormentor and I believed he had the power to extinguish my life if he wanted to. I had to get away.

9

The Damage Done

My alcohol consumption was always an issue. As an adult I spent many of days intoxicated, numbed. It had crept up on me. I was drinking six beers, then ten, then fourteen and eventually four cartons a week. It was always beer followed by the occasional Jack Daniels. I would be regularly drinking 96 bottles in a week just to find equilibrium. My evenings would all end with me passed out on the lounge. My second Wife; Carol was patient with me. She put up with the urinating in the wardrobe and the sleepwalking and the absent partner in the drunken stupor, but it was driving her crazy.

I suppose I had only considered alcohol a problem when it leads to violence. My Father would break his children's bones when he was drunk. I would just pass out so for years I probably didn't realise what an issue it was. I drank for thirty- five years without a hangover. I went to work every morning, did my Fatherly and family duties and my memory stayed sharp. It took my Wife to threaten to leave me for me to ever consider giving up the brown bottle and it took until December 2015 for me to finally break away. I had been hiding in alcoholism and it was time to face myself.

The drunkard was just an extension of the hurt little boy. I was hiding from the men who had treated me less than human. I had shut down the memories of being bullied and abused and tried to drown them in beer. My life was different now. I had a Wife that loved me and I had started to understand love myself. As a young man, sex had been love. I had been a player, a whore, a satyriasis. I had spent years picking up as many women as I could as though I could find something meaningful in quantity. I had been married twice and unfaithful in both relationships. Now as an adult, a Father, a grandFather it was time to be brave enough to admit that sex was also an addiction, a way for me to hide my fragility and to avoid my demons.

Carol was the love of my life. Eventually, I had come to completely trust her and tell her the truth about me, even my unfaithfulness to her. It took her a long time to forgive me. She was brave, I was brave. I had hidden my past so well that I had even lied to doctors who without a reason for my poor mental health had sent me for shock treatment and had even considered that I had brain damage. The medical profession found it easy to label me. I had borderline personality. I was depressed, I was a fungicidal alcoholic. I carried the why all along and the labels were no use whilst I hid the cause. The reason I was in such a ragged state was my childhood experiences and Carol was the first person to hear them in full. I had never trusted someone else enough to share them.

In front of Carol, I was able to explain the depression, guilt, shame, self-blame, eating disorders, anxiety, dissociative patterns, repression, denial, sexual, and relationship problems. I didn't use the confession to talk my way out of the fact I had hurt and betrayed her but I did owe her the truth, the whole ugly truth about who I had been, what I had done and what had been done to me.

Like many survivors of childhood sexual abuse, I had post-traumatic stress disorder. Commonly this leads to difficulties with affection and intimacy, compulsive sexual behaviour, promiscuity, problems concerning desire, arousal, and flashbacks. Some survivors may have dissociated to protect themselves from experiencing the sexual abuse. As adults, they may still use this coping mechanism when they feel unsafe or threatened.

It was very painful to acknowledge the guilt I felt. I carried shame, fear, and embarrassment. I found getting close to people impossible and in all my relationships there would be a lot of loneliness, preventing me from experiencing and learning about intimacy and trust. Of course, I would immediately look for the next relationship hoping this one would fulfil me but I carried the deficit, I carried the issue and until I worked that out no relationship would work.

This journey to truth has been difficult for me and

Carol. I am not all the way home by a long way and even as I write down my story I can occasionally disassociate and revert to me at seven years old. He can take over and take the story off down dark and twisted roads under the cover of pitch-black hail swollen clouds. The lightening that is about to strike could send him cowering for cover, but I want to tell him there are some spots of sunshine on this path. There is the love he feels for his children, the love of his Wife. There is the moment that he takes control and starts to commit words to the page. I want to reassure him and support him to keep walking.

He has a lot of darkness to endure. He will wet the bed and be punished for it. He will be forced to wear his wet clothes on wrapped around his head and face. He will be degraded and told he doesn't count.

The little boy will start to believe he is bad and seek out his own punishment. Low self-esteem will blossom into full-on self-hatred. The child will cut and injure himself; he will seek out experiences with danger and pain and eventually he will attempt suicide. If anyone offers him genuine love or friendship, he will reject it as not being worthy.

Of course, I didn't feel worthy. I was the son of the devil after all. When I was sixteen, I was so concerned about the poison I might pass on to future generations I asked three times to be sterilised. I was terrified I would be the husband and Father that I had endured, and I didn't want to take that risk. Each time the doctor refused on the basis that I was too young. I was so angry. Imagine if I had given my parents grandchildren and then allowed them into their lives. I am so relieved that I did eventually have children and found it easy to love and impossible to harm them. The high points of my life are where I proved that I was not my Father.

I was in a psychiatric hospital for two years. I attended five days a week for two hours. I was immediately identified as a high-suicide risk. I guarded my past in that environment, and it took staff weeks to get slithers of information out of me. I was so tough, so battle-hardened that I was a challenge to even the most skilled professional. My early years had seen me small, timid and eager to please. I was polite and quiet at first and prone to tears. Over the years I had become a storm. A rage accompanied by the smell of brimstone. There were fifty-six years of trauma to unpick. That's why this is a job I haven't completed. I write and relive some of the experience. I write and expose the pain to hopefully pack it away one final time.

I first attempted suicide at the age of twelve. Then I tried again in 1966 by hanging myself. My last attempt was in 2015 when I took an overdose. I am not certain how I haven't been successful, but I am tremendously grateful to still be alive. I have tried to take my life not just to end the pain but also, like a lot of victims, I feel guilt for what happened. I feel the need to say sorry. I am still the boy who is timid, polite and eager to please. I thought that taking my life might make amends for something I had done to deserve my experiences. Perhaps that is what propelled my Father to take his own life in 1977.

I am, however, still alive. I am not my Father and I will stay and face and admit the bleakest moments of my life because all I know is that they weren't my fault. Sober, faithful and honest there is now a chance that the truth will set me free.

10

Men and Monsters

In Glandore sex was the currency. There was always going to be homosexuality where, so many same-sex people are locked away together and so many of them are vulnerable and looking for love, support and connection. I am not ashamed of anything I did in Glandore. I looked after my Brothers and they looked after me. I had been sexualised by Bartlett at age seven and it was all I knew. The boys had a pecking order, were taught to use sex as power and in truth, it was our only bargaining tool.

Nevertheless, we were Brothers and when one of our number was selected by the staff, we would receive them back covered in blood and shit and hysterical and do our best to comfort and patch them up. We would offer spare sheets, clothes and pyjamas. There were even occasions where we organise hunger strikes to protest our abuse but always our show of strength and unity would be futile. The officers became quite systematic in their abuse. One officer would like us up in the shower and demand that we masturbate each other whilst he looked on. There was a discomfort, a shame in this but it wasn't as bad as being the sole victim.

Often boys would be returned with bruises all over their backs and buttocks, with damage to their wrists from bindings. If you made a complaint to a member of staff who wasn't involved in the sexual abuse you would get called a liar and your bruises would have cane marks added to them.

Officers took boys to the kitchen and the dormitory. They got brazen and were often observed by other boys. We knew that new boys would be targeted, and we knew we could do little to protect them. Some of the older boys decided to take revenge. One evening we heard that ten of the boys had hidden their identity by wrapping jumpers around their heads and had set about an officer. He stood no chance and was left bruised and bloody. The police were brought in and anyone who was charged would be sent to Magill boy's home for their sentence. We all kept our mouths shut and the older boys remained anonymous.

The officer was off work for a while but when he returned, he decided to conduct his own enquiry. He took a boy from my dormitory and punched and kicked him until he was hospitalised. Glandore couldn't cover this up and the police did charge the officer who ended up being sacked.

There were five dormitories in total. Each slept twenty boys. Two dorms housed the pre-pubescent boys, aged 5 to 12 and this was called the cottage. There was always a young officer employed to cover the night shift, one in each dorm. Many of them would have day jobs too and were there to make extra money. Somewhere there to prey on the children. We all witnessed blood in the younger boy's bed, and we all heard screams at night. The truth is that you tried desperately not to be a witness. Witnesses were often beaten just to remind them to not talk. The cycle of abuse was passed on as older boys would also visit the younger boys in their dorm. Sometimes they would take them back to their beds with them. It wasn't an especially hidden thing. The staff knew, and it was just another atrocity to ignore.

Drugs also circulated freely, especially cannabis. The officers offered drugs as a reward and the boys were keen for any sort of escape. Drugs were used to get you to comply to sex, or drugs were used to hire older boys as henchmen for the officers to force the younger boys to comply. This sick power structure ran through the institution. The strong would survive and the weak would be used. The boys helping the officers had identified a way to step out of the position of victim. It was the only way they could gain any power.

I was never able to inflict savagery on anyone. I couldn't be bought for booze, cigarettes or drugs. My heart was just too gentle for the dog-eat-dog daily survival. I would always be prey, I wasn't alone. There were lots of boys who were powerless and brutalised by staff and other children. I wonder if any of them survived to live a good life. I wonder if any of them dealt with their pain.

I remember Robert who at fifteen was still sucking his thumb at night and crying for his Mother. He had lost his parents in a car accident. There was also a boy named David who was dying and seemed to be happy about it. He was expecting heaven would be his escape from hell. He had no family and was jealous of mine even after I told him about my Dad. My parents spent time with him on visits. He died after four or five months of being in the home. I prayed for him although I was jealous of the attention he had from my family. Another boy cut his wrists and plenty more escaped at every opportunity. The police would always catch the escapees and deliver them back for a beating.

I thought I had escaped where I was admitted to the psychiatric hospital, but it was there that I met Peter. He was a nurse, a tall man with a comb-over hairstyle from premature balding. He was in his mid-thirties and spoke softly with a stutter. He was a feminine man when I think about it but everyone thought of him as gentle and kind. He professed to being passionate about helping kids with problems and he wanted to help me. He asked me to help him with his magic show and we travelled together, to of all places, Port Pirie. On the way back he took me to a hotel for a meal and offered me some vitamin tablets. I was still so naïve and trusting I took them without thought.

Later that evening I woke to find Peter naked and

on top of me. It took all my effort to fight whatever he had given me to struggle out of bed. I left my clothes in the room and ran out naked to make my escape. Peter had two young sons and was a scout leader. He begged me not to tell anyone and I didn't for fifty years. By the time I did talk about Peter enough time had passed for him to escape prosecution. What could I do? Forgive him? I had to learn to forgive myself.

I was sexualised so early on in my life it would be one of the only ways I could connect to other humans. I had some experiences with women probably too early on in my development, but I had searched these out and enjoyed them at the time. I met an Aboriginal girl who lived with a white family near Glandore. I would sneak into her house and we would have sex in secret. I remember she spoke and dressed beautifully and was an oasis in the brutal world of the boy's home then one day she had just moved on and I didn't see her again. Then there had been a time when I was around twelve and back home in Pirie for a short while. I had a mate called John of the same age, He had great buck teeth and a funny laugh. John's Dad had taken off but he lived with his mum and Sister Janet. Janet had been in a car accident and was in and out of hospital. I went to call on John and he was out, but his Mother had invited me in. She must have been in her late twenties. She was very beautiful and blond, and she persuaded me out of my trousers. It was my first blow job and I excitedly told my Brother. I was a child, but I didn't feel abused. I went back for more and when Janet returned from hospital, I also had sex with her whilst her Mother watched. It may seem weird or grubby, but it was just sex and it was so much less painful than what the men at Glandore offered. Janet became a regular girlfriend eventually, one of many admittedly. We split because her Mother would still make a move on me whenever I was around. I was not to see Janet for a couple of years until I met her in the dentist when I was around nineteen. She had a moustache and was going through a sex change. We went for coffee and I kissed her and wished her all the best. We had been **infatuated as** children. Probably both of us were used and sexualised too early on for our wellbeing but there was a connection there, a sensitivity that we had both craved and now we had to continue with difficult journeys. I hope she became whom she needed to be.

11

City of Churches and Little Deaths

Like plenty of nights before my Father came back from the Pirie hotel drunk and made a beeline for me. He dragged me out of bed and threw me into the car. He demanded to know why people respected me, he demanded to know who I really was. I was a child baffled by my Father's drunken interrogation.

It transpired that some man at the hotel had read about my story in the paper and decided to take issue with my Father. Everyone knows your business in a small town and this man had offered my Father some payback.

When the revenge was finally delivered my Father was hospitalized for three days and he hastily made the decision that we would leave Pirie and head to Adelaide. Even though it was to escape judgment for my beating I was still excited about a new house, in a city with a new sort of life attached.

I am relieved that the house in Northfield has been pulled down. I am sure misery had seeped into the walls and happiness would be impossible for anyone who lived there. I remember the excitement of moving to Adelaide. I remember seeing the city lights as we drove down from the hills. I was naïve enough to believe in fresh starts. Perhaps we were going to be the family I imagined we could in Adelaide.

I planted two trees in the garden at Northfield and they still stand. They have outlasted the house, my Father and will probably outlast me.

We moved into the house with all our dark secrets. My Mother had perfected her veil. She was the dutiful Wife and Mother, the partner of her daughter's rapist. I wonder if she believed the move would afford her a new life.

I was finding out new ways to play out my pain. I was already cutting myself with razor blades and killing birds with mouse traps. I talked to a psychiatrist about this in later life. I knew it was the sort of early signs psychopaths exhibit. I wonder if I was on the path to serial killer at some stage.

I was getting a little braver by this stage. I was always small and slight, and I was fast too. I started to taunt my Father knowing that I could outrun him. My Father would store up all his anger for the few occasions he would get a hold of me. I knew I was provoking him but then my existence seemed to provoke him. I had to find some way to gain some control and I suppose by exploiting my ability to aggravate him I was.

My Father would hurt me but humiliation seemed

to play an increasing part of his behaviour. He would remove my clothes and throw me out of the house. Beatings were always accompanied by my nudity and quite often I would be outside wearing only bruises and dry blood. I would have to wait in the yard until he went to sleep and then my Mother would let me back in. Sometimes he would taunt me through the window, call me a little girl.

I was used to this public nudity. Neighbours had been taking me in for years. I was getting tougher and I felt no shame. It was about this time I was able to gain a little independence selling newspapers in front of the AMP building in Adelaide. I was able to sustain this job whilst I was in and out of Glandore, back home and even on the streets. I would spend my wages on day trips with my Brother. We went fishing, to the football and cricket and we escaped our Father.

What I thought was freedom and independence the authorities called running wild. I was sentenced to go to Winda Boys' Home by the courts. Winda was right next to Glandore and I could talk to mates out the window whilst I was locked inside. The proximity to Glandore also meant that the two institutions shared some staff. At Winda, there was a fat, deaf officer with a face like a beetroot who loved to get us to masturbate and another who stank and liked to make him watch him masturbate. They were just the same predators as Glandore. Then the courts suggested I attend another institution. St. Corinne's Day Clinic was to help me with my mental health. St Corinne's was just another paedophile paradise. I wasn't going to get any help from anyone, and I had come to accept it.

As a teenager my sexual appetite was unassailable. I would be picking up seven girls a week and trying to get my fix three times a day. I picked up a lot of nurses. They were always older than me and sometimes brought dope and alcohol. It was natural for me. I had been sexually active from seven and I thought I'd find all I was missing through sex. I had sex in all sorts of venues in Adelaide from the Drive-in to the car parks to the riverbank. I also took women back home and my Mother would often interrupt me with an older woman.

When I took on my first flat, I started a relationship with a 42-year-old who lived next door. She seduced me but I was happy to go along for the ride. I was never disrespectful to women. I tried to treat them well, but I wasn't in it for the long ride. Sex was a quick fix that only satisfied me for a moment. I would have to be on the lookout for the next hit as soon as it was over.

I wasn't careful and it's possible I could have other children out there or perhaps I put a woman through the pain of an abortion without my support. I'm not proud of my sexual conquests. I know they came from a place of loss.

My Mother and Brother came over to my flat to

inform me that my Father had died. They told me
that the police had informed them that morning
and that he had not left a note. It should have been
the happiest day of my life, but I was numb. I felt
robbed. I lost it at the funeral home, and I lost it at
the cemetery. I fell to the ground as if grief had
paralysed me. I was overwhelmed and had to admit
that I loved this man. The weight of that
threatened to crush me. There was also the fear
that I would be my Father in time and perhaps this
showed me how I would meet my end, at my own
hands, alone.

More than all these feeling was the stark fact that I
would never have justice, revenge or even an
apology. I had such good people around me; my first
mum and dad-in-law were brilliant and offered me
so much love and support. There were emotions I
couldn't control or hide. I was obviously fragile and
obviously a seven-year-old all over again. I just
wanted my Father to love me. I was wondering
what I had done to disappoint him, what I had done
to make him end his life. How was I such a burden
that he had needed to drive out of town and feed
the exhaust fumes through the driver's window? At
what point did he decide to do that, and did he ever
doubt his resolve on that short journey?

I had to retrieve my Father's car. The battery was
flat and Norm, my Father in law, and I went to tow
it home. It stank of death and the exhaust fumes
penetrated my clothes. At one point I stopped the

car, stripped of all my clothes and just walked away. I was picked up by the police and luckily not charged. I was naked again on account of my Father, but he wasn't there to insult me.

12

The Great and the Good

I first met Don Dunstan when I was seven years old in 1961. He came to Glandore at Christmas time. I didn't know who he was or indeed anything about the government of South Australia. At that point, Dunstan would have been sitting on opposition to Playford and about to become the state's most powerful man but to me, he was just another adult at the concert who would eagerly play with us boys. Don loved us boys and we loved Don. I enjoyed sitting on his knee. I was desperate for any form of affection and I didn't scrutinise his motivations at all.

Dunstan was cocky, brash and ambitious. Between the ages of 12 and 16, I spent quite a bit of time in his company I remember him being lean with thick dark hair and a natural confidence. I had reconnected with Dunstan as I was selling newspapers in the city. I also got to know Kevin Crease, the newsreader, because he worked as Dunstan's press secretary. I had rubbed shoulders with Crease in St Corrinne's psychiatric hospital. I was sent there by my Mother for my sex addiction and Kevin Crease was seeing the same psychiatrist as me. I remember the psychiatrist as a quietly spoken man with innate sadness. Kevin was a great talker and had wonderful stories about his days in television.

When I was surviving as a street kid it was not uncommon for a few of us to get invited over to Dunstan's house. Here we could access alcohol and drugs and I met up with Crease again.

It is my belief that there was a paedophile ring in South Australia that had connections with Glandore Boys' home, Winda Boys' Home, St Corrinne's Psychiatrist Hospital, The Methodist Church and Don Dunstan's parliament. The enquiries to this point have scraped the surface of an institutional evil and my story overlaps with state-wide corruption, cover-ups and scandal. I have given my evidence and testimony as have countless others and there has been compensation payouts and even apologies. The full and frank truth is a long way from being told.

I know there are bodies. Those who made it into adulthood where the pain caught up with them and they succumbed to their own destruction, those who used everything at their disposal to numb what they felt until numb became a permanent condition. There are also those who didn't survive their childhood. I am certain there are people buried metaphorically and literally in the ugliness of the near past. I survived, and I owe my Brothers the chance to be recognised as I tell my story.

The state put away seven million dollars to

compensate the victims of its 'care'. I have given evidence, been cross-examined by high court judges, spoke at the royal commission in 2013 and made my peace with the lack of truth and justice on offer. I gain comfort from my belief and the knowledge that God dispenses the final reckoning and those that avoided trial through old age, ill-health, senility or death will be held accountable in the afterlife for their sins on earth.

I contacted the police fifty years after I had been the victim of the crimes. I was able to make statements with real detail. I could still remember Bartlett's features, his large hands and unyielding manner. He is a portrait in terror even now. The passing of time and his poor health saved Bartlett from facing his accuser.

I choose to believe in a Christian God who has walked with me all my life. He shared my path and pain and made sure that I would survive. In return, I have given my whole life to him. I know my life is not just about my life but also the people I mix with on the way. I will one day know why my Father was put on this earth for and why I had to walk the path I did. That, after all, is faith, I lack some specific answers, but I still believe.

I managed to quit drugs when I was twenty. I had my faith and I had developed a strength and resilience that would see me through to adult life. Early on in my teens, I was already standing up to my Father. I was able to think for myself and conceive of a time that he wouldn't be my master. I knew eventually freedom and peace would be mine.

This lack of control aggravated my Father even more. The beatings escalated with my growing confidence but so did my ability to survive them. I remember telling my Brothers and Sisters that this hell wouldn't last forever. I remember telling them we would survive and how this undermined and terrified my Father.

My Mother was a lousy housekeeper, and this too would come to an end. I told my siblings that we could solve all our problems by moving out. We could all have happy, calm, pleasant houses where nobody used their fists or turned a blind eye to it.

Did I care that I would be abandoning my Mother? Not really. She had already abandoned us, her children. Luckily for her, she was liberated herself in 1977 by my Father's suicide. Within four weeks she was in a relationship with another man. My Mother lived with he knew partner for over twenty years until he died. I had a good relationship with Nick, but I found it hard to understand how my Mother had acted. Now she is dead I just hope she finds forgiveness and peace in the afterlife.

My twin. Peter Mathew Sheriff, died on Friday 13th June 1980. I was Peter, he was me, We were one spirit and part of me died with him that day. Pete had been taller than me and with deep blue eyes and shoulder-length hair. I was watching the news on Channel 9 when they reported a fatal car crash.

All six people in the car were killed and I just knew it was him. We had a beautiful connection for all his short life. He had known my first marriage was in trouble and he had come to me a few days earlier to see if I wanted to go on a trip with him. It was organised by some church where they spoke in tongues. He also asked my younger Brother to join him. Neither of us had been able to go and Peter had gone alone.

I went to the hospital to see him and I was able to hold his hand. I was destroyed by the loss of my twin. I must have faith that this is all part of God's plan and that Pete died young so that his kindness was rewarded with heaven.

13

Family

I met Carol thirty-five years ago on a blind date. I knew it was going to be the most significant relationship of my life. I knew from the first day I would marry her.

I have caused my Wife a lot of pain. Carol has had to contend with the old me and the difficult birth of the new me. She has had to put up with my drinking, my pain, my chaos and anger. She has had to put up with me loving her too. Carol asked me to go out into the street and scream to the world that I loved her. I whispered it into her ear and then explained that she was my world. I have six children, four with Carol and two from my previous marriage.

I lost contact with my eldest son, Mark from my first marriage, my fault, my abandonment after the difficulty of splitting from his Mother. I loved him though. I could remember him as a beautiful baby with long eyelashes. When I reconnected, I found out I had two grandchildren? He and his partner Sally have gone on to produce three daughters and I now have two great-grandchildren. My second son from that marriage has issues with drugs and I felt I had to protect the rest of my family and break off contact. I know he carries a hatred for me. I love him and can recall what a happy little child he was.

I know my family have suffered because of my mental illness. My Wife, my children and grandchildren probably suffered because I tried to bottle it up and hide it. Since I have decided to be open and deal with it I hope I hurt them less.

When my third son was born in 1982, he was the apple of my eye. He slept between me and my Wife I took a year of work so that I could care for him. He started walking when he was nine months old and followed his Mother everywhere and when she was pregnant with our first daughter if she had morning sickness, he would pretend to be queasy too. He was a good kid, bright, capable and sporty. He joined the army and then the police force. I am proud of him and so glad I can let him know. Robbie has given me two grandchildren. When I went to see his marching out parade, I sobbed uncontrollably with pride. I remember thinking what a good man he was already, so much better than me. I had my first daughter in 1984 and then Carol and I had a daughter number two in 1987. Hayley was named after the comet that passed over in 1984. Kellie is also a special person. I think of them both as my Princesses and I am always reduced to tears at family events because of my love and pride for them. I was almost hysterical at Hayley's wedding. Our final child and son were born in 1988. My youngest boy Jarryd works with me. In fact, he leads the business and has a great work ethic which I also had but he is another man who has qualities his Father lacked.

I have always been confrontational. I am not violent, but I am someone who has carried a lot of anger and who reacts without thought sometimes. I am learning to manage that, to be a better man and hopefully people have noticed.

It has taken me 62 years to get to the place I am now. My Carol is a natural inspiration. I think she can move the world. After 35 years of marriage, I realise that I was trying to do it all alone and I would never achieve. I reached out for Carol and I accept everything God has to offer.

My children are a gift. All of them are so different but I love them unconditionally and I know that they give my life meaning. Mark, Robbie, Kellie, Hayley and Jarryd I hope I am a good Father and I hope I am not my Father's son.

I have been back to Port Pirie. The last time I was brave enough to face the old house. It was for sale again, freshly painted. Not all my memories of Pirie are bad. I will never go back to Glandore. I am still haunted by the place. I did find myself on the road there one day looking at a civil construction job. As soon as I realised where I was, I began to spin out of control and the terrified child part of me emerged. Glandore is hell. I have no need to revisit it.

As my Wife, Carol and I walk into the sunsets of our life's. I thank God; I feel we have done our duty and as a parent, I can say I am proud of my children. I am in a good place now. I am slowly coming to terms with the hurt little boy. It wasn't his fault.

———————

About Robert Sherriff

AUSTRALIAN ACTOR BORN 8/7/1954

Actor-Poet Author-Singer- Historian

Part of Wolf Creek TV series 2015

Part of Movie 'Maurice's Symphony' 2015

Motivation Speaker

Movie - Snuff 2016

Movie - CULT 2016

Email robsherriff871954@gmail.com

Phone no. +61 (0)466246021

They say you cannot control your destiny this is bullshit. You know and so do I.

But then again, your destiny does not control you. You do. We can make changes. Or you make it happen.

Nothing is impossible. If you want it that bad. Don't let people or numbers a person who can rise above every control you. You are your own person.

Throughout my adult life, I would try and re-write my unhappy childhood to a happy life a full life with meaning, direction.

Love for my Wife and Children.

Mark

My Oldest Son Mark from my First marriage I would not blame him if he hates me I have let him down time after time. I do not blame him. I was so sorry. I love him. He was a beautiful baby boy; his eyelashes were so long. And he was such a happy baby. When I broke up with the first wife, I did not see him for years. I had abandoned him. For a lot of reasons. For so many years. I finally tracked him down by ringing the courts I said I was him I had speeding fines, and they gave me his address. I went to his house. There was no one home. I went home I was in the shower when my wife got home. I was crying my eyes out. We did catch up. I then saw them at their house, and I found out I had two Grandchildren. That was 1999. He has a partner Sally, she is his soul mate, and she is a great Mum, kind and funny. I have a lot of respect for her she understands me they have given me three beautiful Granddaughters and two Great Grand Children. xx

My Second Son from my First Marriage

One Son I have disowned he threatened to kill his Brothers and Sisters about 2001. In life, I told him you could take the Safe Road or the wrong Road. I have nothing to do with him he has lost himself in his little-festered world. He was such a happy little kid. He would laugh all the time, and he had the biggest giggle. When I finally saw him again after so many years he was this freaked out a monster on drugs I think? One day he came to my house and asked me to take him somewhere I said no. Next minute he threatened to kill his step Brothers and Sisters I said from this day I would disown him as he was jealous of what he could see that they had, and he wanted it as well. I would, and I tried I loved him so much but what was I meant to do I had to protect his Brothers and Sisters I love them as much, and it was my duty of care as a Parent to draw that line in the sand. The line that would change his history and send him into an anger of hate for me a hate so strong I would have to watch my back.

A priest I know attacked me personally, he who is without sin throws the first stone?

My Mental Illness

My mental illness if that's what you call it that I have had to overcome in many ways. Has many ups and downs it's like I have a revolving door. I cannot hide behind; a roller coaster rides or a plane in freefall spiralling out of control. Or a train dangerously speeding on an unstable track. I'm just trying to stop all that all those people I love who have gone on this same roller coaster. Remember it's easy to judge sometimes it's better if you can just help.

There was Hurt and frustration, anger and that was deeper more and foreboding that have left my friends family fearing the worst it affected my Wife bad, and my beloved Children who could not understand like the rest of the World did not understand I was too embarrassed to talk about it.

I was locked up for my safety

I am sorry for the pain it caused my wife and children

At last, I think my mind and I are one. On the way, back to one mind, in time.

But then?

Dedication, Thanks and Acknowledgements

This Book I have Dedicated to My Wife and Children and Grandchildren.

My Great Grandchildren. ...You are the Brightest Lights in the Darkest Night.

I dedicated this book to all my good Friends and my "Enemies".

"Enemies" not of my choosing only from their thoughts.

"See no evil, hear no evil, and speak no evil."

"To my Children"

I KNOW MORE THAN I CAN TELL YOU AND CAN'T SAY TO YOU MORE THAN I KNOW

To all my dearest friends we may not see each other for weeks months or years but you are always in my thoughts. Friends are your Family we all have differences of options but at the end of the day were there for each other. I have made lots of mistakes. I have tried to have a heart my life is full of secrets I dare not even share with you have support me and a lot of times I have shut the door most of you have been on this trip with me where I have also caged myself of from this world where I still fear a fear without an end an end that is no stop to all those who have gone out of their way in regards to Wards of State, thank you. Robert. I'm so sorry.

This book is also dedicated to these two medical professions from South Australia.

They have brought me back from no were land a land where I was blinded I could not see.

The pain the hurt my insanity they gave me hope they treated my brain my body and soul. All the medical problems that I have now, and I have lots) are all related to the sexual abuse and domestic abuse. The thing that gave me the most hope was God. The Father loves me for who I am. The thing I hate is political correctness. I am old fashion, yesterday year.

My Psychiatrist (Doctor Arthur Loukas) His words and coffee get up Rose Park.

Phone no. +61 (0)884315833.

Doctor Sanjeev Sabharwal. This man is a true gentleman. Great Doctor. Modbury North.

Phone no. +61 (0)882647824

Kevin and Alanna Armstrong

Rob (Westy) and Peggy Westwood

Rob Amison (Ammo) Belle, Mitchell, Nick

Joe Pillen

Adam Sherwood

Calum Park

Geoff Whatley

Pete and Alison and Taylor, Riley Van der Hoven
Bev Hill

David Kennyworth

Keith and Tania Hamilton

Tammie Alex and Josh Hamilton

Mick and Chris Wills

Mark and Simone Cetinich

Fred Warner

To My dear friend David Chapple who guided me in writing my memoir. XXX

The most amazing song ever written:

Amazing Grace

Available worldwide from

Amazon and all good bookstores

————————

www.mtp.agency

www.facebook.com/mtp.agency

@mtp_agency

9 781912 639335